DANIEL'S DINOSAURS

A TRUE STORY
OF DISCOVERY

Charles Helm

Photography by Charles Helm

Illustrations by Joan Zimmer

Maple Tree Press Inc.
51 Front Street East, Suite 200, Toronto, Ontario M5E 1B3
www.mapletreepress.com

Distributed in Canada by Raincoast Books
9050 Shaughnessy Street, Vancouver, British Columbia V6P 6E5

Distributed in the United States by Publishers Group West
1700 Fourth Street, Berkeley, California 94710

We acknowledge the financial support of the Canada Council for the Arts, the Ontario Arts Council, the Government of Canada through the Book Publishing Industry Development Program (BPIDP), and the Government of Ontario through the Ontario Media Development Corporation's Book Initiative for our publishing activities.

ONTARIO ARTS COUNCIL
CONSEIL DES ARTS DE L'ONTARIO

Dedication
For Linda, who makes everything possible

Acknowledgments
Thanks to Deborah Griffiths for the idea of this book, and to Albert Broeksma, Daniel and Glyn Hewson, Erina Helm, Jenni Lean, and the Hulley and Pitcher families for advice on the initial manuscript.

Exploring and uncovering Tumbler Ridge's fossil heritage (and securing the funding for the resulting projects) has always been enthralling, and at times exacting. Thank you to all who have shared in this passion, including Al Durand, Brian Pate, Wayne Sawchuk, and Kevin Sharman, whose exciting discoveries formed pivotal moments in this process.

Working with Anne Shone, Sheba Meland, and Victoria Hill of Maple Tree Press has been an enriching experience beyond all expectation.

The contributions of Phil Currie and Rich McCrea to this book, Tumbler Ridge, and British Columbian paleontology have been profound. Thank you for all this, but especially for the gentle way you have coaxed and inspired the kids.

Cataloguing in Publication Data
Helm, Charles, 1957-
   Daniel's dinosaurs : a true story of discovery / Charles Helm ; Joan Zimmer, illustrator.

ISBN 1-897066-06-6 (bound).—ISBN 1-897066-07-4 (pbk.)

1. Dinosaur tracks—British Columbia—Tumbler Ridge—Juvenile literature. 2. Dinosaurs—British Columbia—Tumbler Ridge—Juvenile literature. 3. Helm, Daniel—Juvenile literature. 4. Paleontology—British Columbia—Tumbler Ridge—Juvenile literature. I. Zimmer, Joan II. Title.

QE861.5.H44 2004   j567.9'09711'87   C2004-900978-8

Design & art direction: Word & Image Design Studio Inc. (www.wordandimagedesign.com)
Illustrations: Joan Zimmer
Photography: All photos by Charles Helm, except page 27, by Shelly Matthews

Printed in Hong Kong

A   B   C   D   E   F

The author's proceeds from this book will be used to support the paleontological projects of the Tumbler Ridge Museum Foundation.

DINOSAUR DREAMS

Most kids only dream of hunting dinosaurs. A few stay involved long enough to become professionals. Such was my fate, following my childhood dream to eventually become Curator of Dinosaurs at the internationally renowned Royal Tyrrell Museum of Palaeontology.

Philip Currie with Daniel Helm.

I consider myself very lucky to have done so many wonderful things with dinosaurs, and have many fond memories of my experiences. These include collecting dinosaur footprints in British Columbia's Peace River Canyon, finding tyrannosaurs in the Badlands of Alberta, and hunting dinosaurs in the Arctic, in the Gobi, and in Patagonia.

One of my more vivid memories is of a nocturnal hunt for dinosaur trackways in 2002 with Charles and Daniel Helm, Rich McCrea, and others from nearby Tumbler Ridge. By day or night, the area is spectacularly beautiful. However, it was pure magic using the low-angled light of lanterns and flashlights to accentuate the shallow dinosaur footprints, many of which were virtually invisible in the strong but diffuse light of the sun. The sound of water from the adjacent stream rushing and tumbling over the rocks, and the surrealistic vision of the lights dancing across the surfaces of the rocks to pick out and reveal the traces of animals that had died many millions of years ago are permanently imprinted in my mind.

"Man," I thought, "what a lucky kid Daniel is. Not only does he live in such a wonderful place, but he has found significant dinosaur fossils at an age when I was only starting to dream about becoming a paleontologist."

This book is a tale of inspiration. Sometimes dreams do come true!

Philip John Currie, MSc, PhD, FRSC
Curator of Dinosaurs, Royal Tyrrell Museum of Palaeontology

Daniel, his mom, his dad, and his younger sister, Carina, lived in a faraway town called Tumbler Ridge, in the foothills of the Rocky Mountains.

In the summer they would go exploring together. They looked for new caves and waterfalls, and hiked to the tops of mountains.

In the winter they would go cross-country skiing together up frozen creeks and through beautiful canyons. One of their favorite ski routes was up Flatbed Canyon. One day they skied to a spot where they found an old abandoned wooden cabin near a big overhanging rock.

As they sat on the ice under this rock having a snack, Daniel said, "Wouldn't it be fun to see what this place looks like in summer?"

Daniel explores the waterfalls of Tumbler Ridge with Carina.

Once the snow was off the ground, Daniel and his family went exploring. After a few wrong turns, they were lucky to find a game trail, which led them through the forest to the old ruined cabin. The big flat rock beside it was bathed in sunshine all day. Beneath it was Flatbed Creek, with rapids leading into a big pool, just ideal for swimming. They decided to call this place Cabin Pool.

After one look at the rapids, Daniel asked if he could bring a tire tube the next time.

Daniel called up his friend Mark to see if he wanted to join him when they returned to the rapids. And so, just a few days later, Daniel and Mark took their lifejackets, helmets, and inner tube down to the creek.

First they practiced on the small rapids above Cabin Pool. Then they decided to tube down the big rapids below the pool. They started off well, bouncing through some exciting waves, but then the tube hit a big underwater rock and Mark fell off.

He was not hurt, and managed to swim to the far shore, pulling Daniel and the tube to safety. They were walking back along some large flat rocks when, at the exact same moment, they both saw something incredible!

Mark wondered aloud: "Could those be. . ."

". . . dinosaur tracks?" suggested Daniel, almost unable to believe what he was seeing.

There, before their eyes, were six hollow spots in a row in the rock. Each of these had unusual corners at one end, which could have been made by toes. Mark noticed that the footprints—if that is what they were—led into the creek where they were covered by a flat rock.

He said to Daniel, "If we take away that rock, we should find more tracks."

Could these shapes in the rock really be tracks left by a dinosaur?

A few days later, Daniel and Mark lifted up a crowbar and heaved it up the rock. Yes! There were two more footprints—just where they had hoped. It seemed clear that this was a trackway—a set of footprints made by a single large animal. They had found a dinosaur!

Daniel (at right) and Mark had always been interested in dinosaurs—and dreamed that one day they might find evidence of dinosaur life. They knew this was a big discovery. The boys managed to get in touch with Rich McCrea, one of North America's top dinosaur footprint experts. Rich was also very excited, and promised to come for a visit the next summer.

That winter there was lots of snow. When Daniel, his mom, his dad, and Carina went skiing up Flatbed Canyon, it was hard to guess what the trackway might look like under all the snow and ice. One night Daniel woke up screaming after a bad dream about the ice destroying the footprints.

Finally, spring came. All the snow melting in the mountains made the rivers fuller than usual, which meant that Daniel and Mark were unable to cross the creek to see if the trackway was still there.

As spring turned into summer, Daniel and Mark became more and more excited about Rich the paleontologist's visit. But a few weeks before Rich was supposed to arrive, it began to rain, gently at first, then harder and harder. It rained steadily for three days and three nights! The rivers all came down in flood, and everywhere it seemed bridges were being washed away. It was the worst flood the area had seen in fifty years, and Daniel and Mark began to despair. What if the force of the flood destroyed the tracks before Rich even got to see them?

Daniel watches the flooding with dread, hoping the dinosaur prints won't be washed away forever.

The water levels slowly went down. Late one night—at last—Rich arrived. Daniel and Mark were quite nervous of him in the beginning, as Rich was such an important person. But very soon he seemed like a best buddy to them. The back of Rich's truck was full of interesting fossil-type stuff and all his shirts had dinosaur pictures on them. When he signed his name, instead of putting a dot on top of the "i," Rich drew a little three-toed dinosaur footprint. He even brought the boys dinosaur CDs.

First thing the next morning, Daniel and Mark took Rich down to their trackway, hoping for the best. The tracks were still there!

"Wow, you guys are good!" exclaimed Rich. "This is the longest dinosaur trackway I have ever seen in this kind of rock. It was made by an ankylosaur."

Hearing this, Mark and Daniel did a few high fives, grabbed each other's arms, and did a strange little dance on the rock.

Daniel and Mark uncovered more of the trackway under Rich's supervision. After lifting off overlying rocks with their crowbars, they used buckets full of water to wash away the mud and expose the footprints.

Ankylosaurs were armored plant-eating beasts, as big as a large rhinoceros, often with clubs at the ends of their tails for defense.

How could Rich tell right away what kind of dinosaur had left these tracks? Rich knew this by spotting something the boys had missed. In front of every clear footprint was a fainter, shallower, smaller print—the trackway had to have been made by a dinosaur walking on all fours. From the pattern of the prints, and the age of the rock they were found in, Rich knew they could only have been made by an ankylosaur. See page 35 to learn how to recognize different dinosaurs' footprints.

Rich and the boys worked hard to find more of the trackway, lifting and removing rocks that lay on top of it. When they had finished, there were twenty-six prints! Rich suggested that they rub a layer of baby powder onto each print to see them more clearly.

Once they had brushed the powder into the prints, Daniel (right) and Mark couldn't believe their eyes. The trackway jumped out at them from the rock, and could now be seen from far away.

The boys helped Rich do some important scientific work on the tracks. First they drew a square-metre (10-square-foot) grid onto the rock with chalk so that Rich could record the site properly and take photographs. Next they traced the footprints onto plastic sheets and measured their length and width.

The team also measured the distances and angles between the footprints. Rich was then able to use a mathematical formula to calculate that this ankylosaur was 1.2 metres (4 feet) high at the hip, and was ambling along at just 2 kilometres (1¼ miles) per hour.

While they were working, Rich knelt down to put his compass on a rock beside the trackway. When the boys had found the tracks the previous year, this rock had been covered by moss, but the flood had washed the moss away.

Suddenly Rich shouted out, "Dinosaur bone!" He told the boys that this was one of the first places in the world where dinosaur footprints and bone had ever been found right next to each other in the same rock layer. This time Rich, Daniel, and Mark all joined together in a longer and even sillier dance!

Rich prepared to remove the bone so that it could be carefully examined in a museum. The next day they worked together at getting it out safely, and after a few hours they were carrying it out of the creek.

Rich's Footprint-Finding Tips

It had been a great visit. Before Rich left, he told the boys his footprint-finding tricks:

- Always look under rock overhangs.
- Focus on rocks with ripple marks.
- Learn the shapes of the common footprints and train your eye to find those shapes in the rocks (see page 28).

Rich also looked at maps of the area with them to help Mark and Daniel decide which canyons to explore next. Rich used the map to find out about the different types of rocks in the area, and then they went looking for dinosaur tracks. was from 225 to 65 million years ago, so they needed to look at rocks of this age. Dinosaurs only lived on land, so they could not have been in rocks that had formed deep in the ocean. Because the Tumbler Ridge area is mostly covered in forest, only in the canyons would there be enough bare rock on the surface for them to see.

Rich used a hammer and chisel to carefully remove rock in the area all around the bone, but a short distance away from it. This is what paleontologists call "pedestaling" a bone (see above left). Next, to protect the bone and the rock encasing it, they covered it with wet tissue paper followed by layers of plaster of Paris. Once this dried Rich could use the hammer and chisel again to easily pop off the pedestaled rock and bone. They turned it upside down, and covered the underside with plaster of Paris. Now the bone was safely "jacketed" and could be carried out.

Once they knew how and where to look, Daniel and Mark and their friends were finding dinosaur evidence all over the place.

In a nearby canyon, there were twenty footprints on the very first rock overhang they looked under. The footprints in this canyon were the first of this age to be discovered anywhere in the world. One amazing footprint showed that the dinosaur had had a broken toe. Another interesting print was made up of fossilized oyster shells. One rare footprint even showed them what dinosaur skin looked like (see below).

Right there on the rock at Cabin Pool, Daniel and Mark helped expose beautiful, deep prints. They helped sweep the rock clean and found there were one hundred and seventy-one footprints on it, made by at least five kinds of dinosaurs! Some had been made by plant-eating ornithopod dinosaurs. Others had been made by meat-eating theropod dinosaurs that were probably chasing the ornithopods. And there were also many ankylosaur tracks.

This ornithopod footprint contains a skin impression, the equivalent of a human fingerprint. The bottom of a dinosaur's foot was covered with scales called tubercles. Only very rarely is the quality of a footprint so good that you can actually see the marks these tubercles made (see close-up inset photo below).

Theropods like this one would hunt and eat plant-eating ornithopods and ankylosaurs.

A clear theropod footprint.

Daniel and Mark sent Rich details of their discoveries by e-mail. The next summer, Rich came back for another visit to see all these exciting new things for himself. Unfortunately, on the day he arrived, Mark and his family were getting ready to move away from Tumbler Ridge.

The very next day was the first field trip, down a deep canyon. Mark was unable to go because he had to do his final packing, but Daniel went on the expedition. Rich was recording everything he saw in his scientific diary. Suddenly, up ahead, he saw a large rock with a big fossil tree trunk in it.

He said to Daniel and the others, "Where there are fossil tree trunks, always look for dinosaur bones, because they are often found together."

It seemed that no sooner were the words out of his mouth, than someone shouted out, "Bones!" Everyone ran over to the rock, and soon they were all finding bones. Daniel found an impressive long bone half sticking out of it.

When he heard about this from Daniel, Mark couldn't believe his bad luck at not having been a part of this successful trip. And the next day he was gone. Daniel was sad that from now on, he would have to do his exploring without his good friend.

Once an important fossil discovery has been made, there is often a sense of urgency to excavate. The material may be vulnerable to weather conditions and floods, as well as to the interest of inexperienced fossil hunters. In order to properly preserve the fossils, paleontologists know they need to act responsibly. Before removing bone and other fossil material from a site, they must first obtain an excavation permit.

Daniel and Rich examine a rock with dinosaur bones at the skeleton site. Why was this discovery so exciting? They had discovered the first ever dinosaur skeleton in the province of British Columbia! Not only that, but at 93 million years old, it was by far the oldest dinosaur ever found in western Canada, and possibly a new species to science.

As time passed, more and more people began to hear about these dinosaur finds. Daniel got to be a busy guy. He and Mark had already talked on the radio and now Daniel was giving interviews to reporters from newspapers and magazines.

Daniel learned that the best way to see the footprints was by using lanterns in the middle of the night. This is because footprints in rock are best seen when the light is slanting, and he could control the light angle with the lantern. Soon Daniel was guiding important visitors on lantern tours at night, and to Cabin Pool and their original ankylosaur trackway by day.

Rich teaches Daniel how to conduct a lantern tour at night.

So much interesting dinosaur and fossil material had been found that work began to build a museum and dinosaur center to put it all in. At the same time, a beautiful hiking trail to Cabin Pool was built for visitors.

Then Daniel got some really, really exciting news. Because these discoveries were so important, Rich was bringing Dr. Philip Currie to stay in Daniel's home. Philip Currie is a world-famous paleontologist. For Daniel, this was more important than a king or queen or president or prime minister coming to stay.

"I'll give him my bedroom to sleep in," he offered.

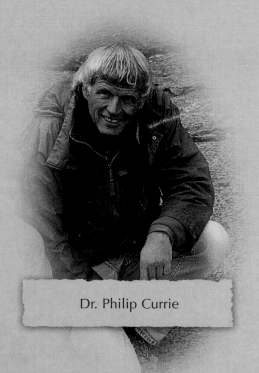

Dr. Philip Currie

Phil Currie is shown the fossilized tree trunk that led to the discovery of the skeleton. Wayne Sawchuk (far right) was the first to spot the dinosaur bones.

When Phil Currie arrived, everyone was a bit nervous, because he is such a famous man. But Phil was not only friendly, he was laid back and keen to help. They took him to the skeleton site. Phil spoke in a soft, deep voice and everyone listened very carefully when he spoke.

"This skeleton is definitely ornithopod, probably either the world's oldest known hadrosaur or else North America's first iguanodontid," Phil said. "And what you folks thought was a dinosaur bone is actually a fossilized turtle shell, the first ever found from this age of rock, and therefore very important. I'll tell my colleague who specializes in turtles."

Fossilized turtle shells (like this one above) look much like shoulder blades or pelvic bones of dinosaurs. Phil used a powerful magnifying lens to help him know for sure. This turtle must have been caught in a flood, and came to rest in the same logjam as the dinosaur.

Ornithopods were one big group of plant-eating dinosaurs. Hadrosaurs (above left), a kind of ornithopod, are also known as "duck-billed dinosaurs." They were very common in the few million years before dinosaurs became extinct, but there are few bones to tell paleontologists when and how they first arose. Iguanodontids (above right) were another big group of ornithopods, first found in Europe.

On the last morning of Phil's visit he asked to be taken to Cabin Pool, and to be shown the trackway downstream that Daniel and Mark had discovered two years earlier. They quickly carried fallen logs out of the forest, and used them to build a bridge over the rapids. For the first time, Flatbed Creek could be crossed without getting wet. Phil and Daniel led the way to the track site.

"Neat trackway, Daniel," said Phil. "Tell me all about how you found it."

And so Daniel told him the whole story. Daniel could not believe how in just two years since he had gone tubing, one thing had led to another as it had. And here he was now telling one of the greatest dinosaur experts in the world all about it.

"So you and Mark started all this off, Daniel. Good job!" said Phil, and he shook Daniel's hand.

Phil crosses Flatbed Creek on the way to the ankylosaur trackway.

Daniel shows Phil the track site.

After Phil and Rich had left, it seemed to Daniel that he was the luckiest boy alive. Many kids dream about finding dinosaurs, and he had lived out his dream. It had all started with footprints. Already Daniel couldn't wait for the next summer, when he would be able to help with the skeleton dig, which he had heard would take a whole two months. He would ask Mark to come back to Tumbler Ridge for his vacation. Together they could maybe be part of the dig team, and would catch up on each other's news.

But life was still busy—too busy sometimes—between his schoolwork, his family, his friends, and all the fuss about these dinosaurs.

So sometimes Daniel, his mom, his dad, and Carina would walk down the trail to Cabin Pool early in the morning, before there were any tourists around. His mom would lie and relax in the sun. His dad would get into weird positions on the rock doing yoga, and his sister would play on the sandy beach beside the pool.

And Daniel would just sit there on the rock and relax. He'd think back—way back—in time, about what the scene may have looked like in the Age of Dinosaurs. With so many footprints so close together on this rock, Daniel imagined it would have been something like a drinking pool in the African savannah, where a whole bunch of different animals came together, and left behind their footprints. It would have been a flat area, with sand and mud, and swamps and forests nearby. There would have been pterosaurs (flying reptiles) in the air and elasmosaurs (long-necked reptiles) in the nearby ocean.

And Daniel would dream about what it may have been like to be a dinosaur there, more years ago than he could begin to imagine.

Time to relax and imagine at Cabin Pool.

Identifying Dinosaurs and Their Footprints

So far, footprints of three major groups of dinosaurs have been found in the Tumbler Ridge area: theropods, ornithopods, and ankylosaurs. Footprints of birds, turtles, and crocodilians have also been found. Here's how to recognize the dinosaurs found at Tumbler Ridge.

Theropod footprints have three main toes on the foot, often showing long, sharp claws. The footprints are usually longer than they are wide, and the trackway is often quite narrow.

Theropods were meat-eating dinosaurs, ranging in size from the very large Tyrannosaurus to the small Procompsognathus. Theropods walked on two legs (bipedal), had sharp claws on their feet and often on their hands, and usually had dagger-like teeth.

Ornithopod footprints have three main toes on the foot. Usually the toes are blunt and hoof-like. The footprints are almost as wide as they are long and the trackway is wider than that of theropods. When forefoot (*manus*) prints are visible they tend to be much smaller than those of the hindfoot (*pes*).

Ornithopods were a group of large, plant-eating dinosaurs that usually walked on two legs, but they could walk on all fours when it suited them. They had very efficient batteries of teeth suitable for grinding tough vegetation. This group includes the hadrosaurs, and the iguanodontids, which gave rise to them.

Ankylosaur footprints have large hindfeet with four toes, which are about as wide as they are long. The forefeet are smaller than the hindfeet, have five toes, are much wider than they are long, and are shaped like a crescent moon. Ankylosaur trackways can be fairly wide.

Ankylosaurs were large, armored, plant-eating dinosaurs. There are two main groups: ankylosaurids, which have a tail club, and nodosaurids, which lack a tail club but have an impressive array of shoulder spikes. The ankylosaurs had small leaf-blade-shaped teeth, which were not suited for chewing or even biting tough vegetation; they preferred to feed on soft-stemmed, herbaceous plants. They were a Cretaceous version of an all-terrain vehicle and the full-sized adults likely had little to fear from any individual theropod. Like sauropods, ceratopsians, and stegosaurs, ankylosaurs walked on all fours (quadrupedal).

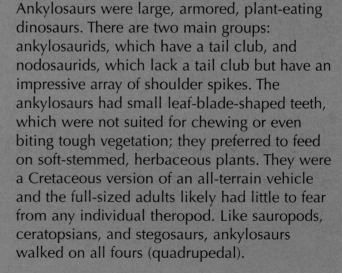

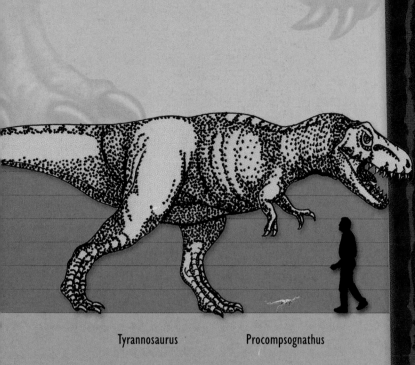

Tyrannosaurus

Procompsognathus

Hadrosaur

Iguanodontid

Nodosaurid

Ankylosaurid

What makes this area so rich in dinosaur footprints? Since millions of years ago, this area (the valley) was just below sea level or close to it. It was in such a position on the earth that the climate was hot. A large river flowed slowly, fed by marshes and swamps.

There were many dinosaurs in this area, including herds, and they moved closely together. In these very large herds, the number of the footprints was very close together, over a period of time in this area. This is known as 'dinoturbation'. There must have been lots of dinosaurs!

How are footprints preserved? If the footprints had dried out, they would not be preserved. They needed to stay moist, allowing a layer of bacteria to grow in them. Then they needed to be covered by sediment (mud, silt or sand) from a flood.

Over millions of years, they were covered by other sediments, which in time became rock, to a depth of up to 100 metres (330 feet). Then lots of water was needed, over a long period of time, to erode away these layers. This could expose the rocks on which the footprints were formed. Scientists think that these rocks get separated more easily from each other just at the level of the footprints, all because of the action of those bacteria so long ago.

In the future, floods will destroy the footprints we can see today and will probably expose new ones.

ABOUT DANIEL'S DINOSAURS

The whole of *Daniel's Dinosaurs* is a true story, and describes the incredible events that happened in Tumbler Ridge in the summers of 2000, 2001, and 2002. Tumbler Ridge is a beautiful, remote community in the Rocky Mountains of British Columbia.

Northeastern British Columbia has been known for over seventy years as one of the best places in the world for dinosaur footprints. But looking into the background of this story allows us to understand just how important Daniel Helm and Mark Turner's discoveries are to the study of dinosaurs.

In 1930, a famous dinosaur hunter named Charles M. Sternberg came to investigate reports of dinosaur footprints in the Peace River Canyon, 100 kilometres (60 miles) to the north of what is now Tumbler Ridge. He wrote about these scientifically for the first time. These tracks, 1700 in all, were almost forgotten until the 1960s and 1970s. That's when the British Columbian government decided to build first one, and then another, enormous dam in this canyon. All the wonderful tracks would be flooded! It was time for a big rescue operation. Many of the best prints were cut out of the rock with rock saws and are now in museums. Philip Currie was in charge of much of this work.

In the other direction, 120 kilometres (75 miles) to the south of Tumbler Ridge, an amazing rock slab was found in the mountains in the 1980s. The rock could only be reached easily by helicopter, but on it were many interesting trackways. One of these was so good that Philip Currie flew in with a *National Geographic* team to film it. When they arrived they discovered that it was gone— the whole rock slab had slid into the river below and shattered!

By the end of the twentieth century, these two important sites had been lost forever. There had been only a few other northern British Columbia footprint discoveries in remote places. Paleontologist Rich McCrea began taking an interest in the area, so Mark and Daniel's discovery couldn't have come at a better time.

For the record book, the Cabin Pool rock has the biggest known collection of prints in British Columbia, and the boys' first ankylosaur trackway is the longest known in the province. Although dinosaur footprints have been found in many parts of the world, the Tumbler Ridge tracks are special for other reasons as well: there is an amazing variety of forms and types of footprints to see within a small area; they are just a short distance from town, easily reached along short hiking trails; and they are mostly on safe, flat, horizontal rock surfaces in dramatic canyons.

The discovery of the skeleton was a real bonus. People have asked what all the fuss is about, as thousands of dinosaur skeletons have been found and excavated in the Badlands of Alberta, British Columbia's neighbor to the east. The answer is all about geological time. The Alberta dinosaurs have been found mostly in rocks that are roughly 65 to 75 million years old; whereas the Tumbler Ridge discovery is in rocks that are 93 million years old. Very little dinosaur bone has been found from this time period *anywhere in the world*.

In the summer of 2003, British Columbia's first dinosaur excavation began, led by Rich McCrea along with paleontologist Lisa Buckley, on behalf of the Tumbler Ridge Museum Foundation. They flew in a large generator and two air compressors by helicopter

and spent six weeks painstakingly taking apart the rock with air hammers and air scribes. Mark returned to Tumbler Ridge for his summer vacation and together the boys found many new tracks and assisted Rich and Lisa with the dig.

Soon it became clear that they were dealing with a lot more than they had originally thought. They found bone in six large blocks in the base of the canyon, and also in four widely separated places in the canyon walls above. This was not just a single skeleton but a dinosaur bone bed in which more than one type of dinosaur could be found, as well as many other fossils. By the end of the season they had identified seventy-five dinosaur bones, ankylosaur and crocodile armor, a turtle jaw, a tooth that came from either a crocodile or a theropod, fish scales, and a rare fossilized pine cone. Philip Currie and his team came for another visit, and estimated that there was enough work at this one site for twenty summers!

Dinosaur fever continues to grip Tumbler Ridge. In 2003, Dino Camps were held for kids aged seven to twelve, and Daniel and Carina were in the first graduating class. The Tumbler Ridge Museum's first dinosaur exhibits were also officially opened, and the original bone that Rich, Mark, and Daniel had found, now prepared and better exposed, was returned to Tumbler Ridge for display. In recognition of their importance, the main dinosaur sites have been given official protection. None of this would have happened were it not for the perceptiveness and perseverance of two young boys.

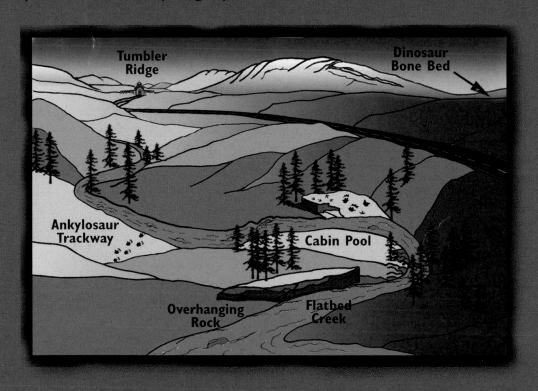